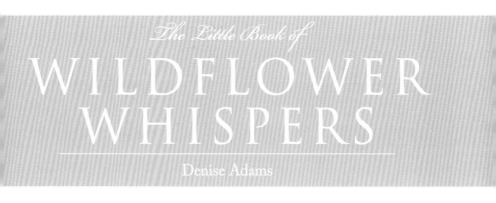

The Little Book of

WILDFLOWER
WHISPERS

Denise Adams

NIMBUS
PUBLISHING
— NIMBUS.CA —

Nimbus Publishing Limited
3660 Strawberry Hill Street, Halifax, NS, B3K 5A9
(902) 455-4286 nimbus.ca

Printed and bound in China

NB1364

All photos by Denise Adams
Design: Jenn Embree
Editor: Emily MacKinnon

Library and Archives Canada Cataloguing in Publication

Title: The little book of wildflower whispers / Denise Adams.
Other titles: Wildflower whispers
Names: Adams, Denise, 1961- author, illlustrator.
Identifiers: Canadiana (print) 20189068191 | Canadiana (ebook) 20189068205 | ISBN 9781771087438 (hardcover) | ISBN 9781771087445 (HTML)
Subjects: LCSH: Wild flowers—Pictorial works. | LCSH: Photography of plants. | LCSH: Mindfulness (Psychology)
Classification: LCC TR724 .A33 2019 | DDC 779/.343—dc23

Nimbus Publishing acknowledges the financial support for its publishing activities from the Government of Canada, the Canada Council for the Arts, and from the Province of Nova Scotia. We are pleased to work in partnership with the Province of Nova Scotia to develop and promote our creative industries for the benefit of all Nova Scotians.

*Wildflowers, no matter their status,
always reward the genuinely curious.*

EARLY SPRING

Treat coltsfoot not as dandelion, but as a joyous harbinger of spring

Pussy willows are sure to cheer the winter-weary heart.

Bring them in from the cold; give early alder twigs a vase and they will thank you with garlands of gold.

Ever so blessed is the mother whose child presents her with a bouquet of mayflowers on Mother's Day.

There is no point in going on a search for wild spring violets;
rather, they find you.

Are not wild azaleas just as impressive as their garden-variety cousins?

Johnny-jump-ups live up to their name;
they pop up just about anywhere.

The most annoying of garden weeds is surprisingly among the most colourful and elegant!

LATE SPRING

Diversity, peace, and plenty; what glorious untamed harmony!

You may consider viper's bugloss a "come-from-away" but truthfully, it's been here far longer than any of your garden flowers.

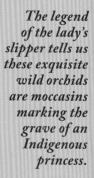

The legend of the lady's slipper tells us these exquisite wild orchids are moccasins marking the grave of an Indigenous princess.

Never pick an azure-coloured lupine—it is the birthplace of and shelter for the endangered Karner blue butterfly.

Three petals, three shadows, three sepals waving.
Everything memorable comes in threes!

Call us not weeds but pretty "flowerscapes" on your lawn!

EARLY SUMMER

And to think that flowers are actually colour-blind!

It has been said that art imitates life, but when it comes to wildflowers, life rather imitates art.

Some wildflowers just can't take "no" for an answer.

A favourite of Queen Marie Antoinette.
Pick as many phlox as you please, have no regrets!

He loves me, he loves me not…. She loves me, she loves me not….
It's never too late to dream of a date.

Twirl and twirl in your pointed shoes and cerise tutu.
Welcome to my yard wildflower ballet!

I think myself far prettier than your needy garden pirouette petunias.
Look at me! Am I not entitled to a little vanity?

Purple loosestrife is guilty of nothing more than being feared.

I found this
wild chicory
living on
the street
and brought
it home for
new friends
to meet.

What could possibly compel someone to dream of a voyage to a desolate, inhospitable red planet devoid of flowers?

Wildflowers have the ability to set roots just about anywhere.

I can't help but admire any flower that mimics the star we call the sun.

MIDSUMMER

What a joy it is to see something unknown from a pack of wildflower seeds return year after year.

Sometimes an invasive wildflower is just what you need to embellish a spot where nothing else will grow.

Surely you remember that irresistible childhood urge to pop these miniature meadow balloons.

I'd rather have colour than a barren stone wall; I'd rather have pretty venom than nothing at all.

No amount of rain can wash away this drop of Queen Anne's blood as she confected such fine embroidery.

Butter and eggs:
a snowshoe
hare's snack,
a hoverfly's
brunch, a deer's
lunch, and—
regrettably—
a hiker's boot
scrunch.

*Fireweed plants are nature's paramedics to damaged soil;
they arrive on parachutes of silk,
stabilize the situation, and tend to the sick.*

Coastal plants have had to evolve very thick skins.

What isn't the norm or doesn't conform gives birth to superstition.

*Turn a walk in the forest into a visit
to the dispensary of the woods.*

You will see constellations in a wildflower only once you've slowed down enough to notice.

While the early morning mist wrapped me in blissful solitude, blue-eyed grass had been surveying my moves the whole time.

LATE SUMMER

Evening primrose works the night shift. It blooms in late afternoon into the cool of night, then takes a long nap shortly after sunrise.

Bull thistle became the floral emblem of Scotland for being a natural barrier that forced the advancing enemy to fall into a deep fjord.

Sometimes, the only way to appreciate tiny wildflowers is to get down to their level.

*Just when
I think the
dandelions
have all by
now expired,
I am faced
with a
sobering
truth....*

Swaths of glitter and gold....
This day, black-eyed Susan,
my heart you stole.

I see the resilience of the wild Canadian lily as homage to the Indigenous peoples of this nation.

Bald is *beautiful.*

*Starwort grows in
ditches and in fields
of hay, yet is elegant
enough to adorn a
bride's veil.*

Roadside yarrow is usually white but to find one blushing,
what a delight!

To come across a little tidal pasture of sea lavender is heavenly.

The fruit of blue bead lily is a standing ovation for triumphant forests.

What a pleasant surprise when a lovely, fragrant wildflower shows up in the garden unannounced.

AUTUMN

These onionskin rosettes from summer to snow are as everlasting as a poem by Edgar Allan Poe.

If I could return as a wildflower, it would have to be water lily.

*A deathbed
of petals…
I was the
only one to
attend the
wake.*

In olden days, mothers and daughters braided their hair before bed.

Goldenrod reminds me of remnant trails of comet tails.

Every garden cultivar—fruit, vegetable, or ornamental shrub and flower—has its ancestry in a wildflower.

To pluck purple aster out as a noxious weed is a gardener's absolute worst misdeed.

Cattails are sentinels guarding the boggy fort:
"No one proceed beyond this point!"

It's that time of year when the snowshoe hare's coat turns from chestnut to white, and gardeners begin their winter respite.

It's the growing season's grand finale!